370

8/03

W9-BSH-052

STARS OF SPORT

EMMITT SMITH

BY KIMBERLY A. GATTO

KIDHAVEN
PRESS™

THOMSON
————— ✦ ————— ™
GALE

San Diego • Detroit • New York • San Francisco • Cleveland
New Haven, Conn. • Waterville, Maine • London • Munich

© 2004 by KidHaven Press. KidHaven Press is an imprint of The Gale Group, Inc.,
a division of Thomson Learning, Inc.

KidHaven™ and Thomson Learning™ are trademarks used herein under license.

For more information, contact
KidHaven Press
27500 Drake Rd.
Farmington Hills, MI 48331-3535
Or you can visit our Internet site at http://www.gale.com

LIBRARY OF CONGRESS CATALOGING-IN-PUBLICATION DATA

Gatto, Kimberly A.
  Emmitt Smith / by Kimberly A. Gatto.
    p. cm. — (Stars of Sport)
Summary: Discusses the life of Emmitt Smith including his childhood, education,
family life, and football career.
  ISBN 0-7377-2084-0 (hardback : alk. paper)
1. Smith, Emmitt, 1969– —Juvenile literature. 2. Football players—United States—
Biography—Juvenile literature. 3. Dallas Cowboys (Football team)—Juvenile liter-
ature. [1. Smith, Emmitt, 1969– .2. Football players. 3. African Americans—
Biography.] I. Title. II. Series.
  GV939.S635G38 2004
  796.332'092—dc22

                                                                      2003013325

Printed in the United States of America

Contents

A Star
Is Born

On May 15, 1969, a boy was born to Emmitt Smith Jr., and his wife, Mary. The baby was named Emmitt James Smith III, in honor of his father and grandfather. The Smith family, which included six-year-old Marsha, lived in a **housing project** in Pensacola, Florida. Emmitt's father worked as a city bus driver, while his mother kept busy caring for the children. Over the years, the Smith family grew to include four more children: Erik, Emory, Emil, and Connie.

Even as a baby, Emmitt seemed to show an interest in football. While his father watched football games on TV, little Emmitt rocked back and forth in his baby swing. His parents soon noticed that whenever an exciting moment would occur in the game, Emmitt would stop rocking and watch the players on the screen.

Emmitt Smith proudly raises his trophy for breaking the NFL rushing record in 2002. Emmitt has been interested in football ever since he was child.

It was no wonder that Emmitt was drawn to football at an early age. In the Smith household, football was an important pastime. Emmitt's father had played both **running back** and defensive back in high school. While knee injuries kept the elder Smith from turning pro, football remained an important part of his life. On weekends, Mr. Smith played for the Pensacola Wings, a local semipro team.

Early Years

When Emmitt was eight years old, the Smith family was able to move out of the projects and into their own home. Mr. Smith had built a small brick house on North G Street, on land owned by his parents, behind their home. The empty lots near the Smiths' new home were wide open, with plenty of room for a game of football. Emmitt and his brothers, along with some cousins and friends, played nearly every weekend. They ran through puddles and dirt, throwing the ball and tackling each other.

When Emmitt's parents realized how much he enjoyed playing football, they signed him up with a local league run by the Salvation Army. Emmitt usually played the quarterback position but was especially talented as a running back. When Emmitt Smith ran with the ball, nobody seemed to be able to catch him.

Family Values

As he grew older, Emmitt became well-known in the junior football leagues throughout Florida. There was only one problem. While he was not tall for his age, Emmitt was much stronger—and bigger built—than most of the other children. By age thirteen, he weighed 180 pounds and was built more like a grown man than a young teenager. As a result of his size, parents and coaches often accused Emmitt of fibbing about his real age. Sometimes they even asked to see his birth certificate.

Emmitt did not let the accusations upset him. His family had given him a deep sense of self-worth. Emmitt was taught from the time he was a toddler to respect others and treat them well. He was not allowed to play football until his homework was complete, and he was encouraged to do his best at anything he tried.

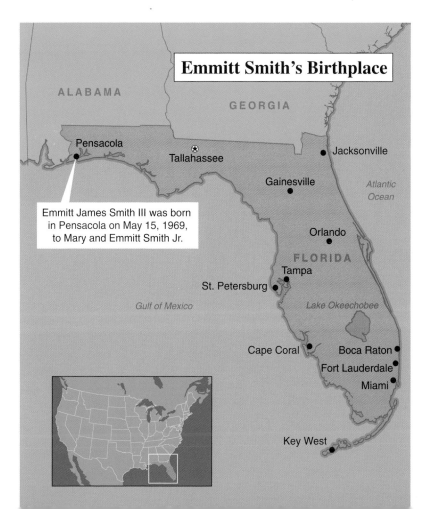

Emmitt Smith's Birthplace

ALABAMA

GEORGIA

Pensacola

✪ Tallahassee

Jacksonville

Gainesville

Atlantic Ocean

Emmitt James Smith III was born in Pensacola on May 15, 1969, to Mary and Emmitt Smith Jr.

Orlando

FLORIDA

Tampa

St. Petersburg

Gulf of Mexico

Lake Okeechobee

Cape Coral

Boca Raton

Fort Lauderdale

Miami

Key West

Emmitt's parents also taught him to help others in need. His grandmother, Erma (called "Mama" by the family), suffered from a disease that had left her paralyzed. Confined to a wheelchair, Mama was no longer able to cook, clean, or even feed herself. Young Emmitt often helped Mama with these things while his grandfather worked nights at a sheet metal factory. Emmitt helped out with the cleaning and laundry, and he talked to Mama when she needed company. "She helped me more than I helped her," Emmitt later said. "As I got

Emmitt skillfully dodges an Arizona Cardinal defender. As a teenager, Emmitt was much bigger than other players his age.

older and looked back on it, I was glad for the experience because it taught me responsibility for someone else. She needed my help."[1]

Dwight Thomas

When Emmitt was not studying or helping his grandmother, he practiced his football skills. One day, a man came to visit Emmitt's eighth-grade football team at Brownsview Middle School. The man, Dwight Thomas, was the new coach of the Escambia High School "Gators." Thomas had come to Brownsview to meet with the students who would be attending Escambia High in the fall. He was hoping to find some new players for his Gators team, which had posted losing records for seven straight seasons.

At Brownsview, Thomas decided to watch the players as they got ready for practice. He noticed that many of the boys wore wrinkled and dirty clothes. When they introduced themselves, the boys looked down and did not firmly shake Thomas's hand. But one student stood out from the rest: Emmitt Smith.

Thomas's first impression of Emmitt was that he was far too mature to be an eighth grader. He was bigger than the others and was dressed in a freshly ironed polo shirt and slacks. Emmitt spoke clearly and gave Thomas a firm handshake. And when Thomas saw Emmitt run with the football, he realized that the young player was quick and strong. Even though Thomas had never started a freshman before, the coach placed Emmitt on Escambia's starting lineup that fall.

Setting Goals

In his first game with Escambia, Emmitt ran like a pro. The Gators were playing against Pensacola Catholic School, which had a much stronger team. Emmitt, one of only two freshmen on the Gators, carried the ball eleven times, for 115 yards and two **touchdowns**. This game broke the Gators' longtime losing streak. By the third game of the season, the Gators were still undefeated, thanks in part to Emmitt's contributions. Emmitt set a personal goal to lead the team to a winning season.

Emmitt easily sidesteps a tackle. As a freshman in high school, Emmitt made the starting lineup of his school's football team.

*Emmitt rushes with the ball past the Atlanta Falcons'
defense. Even in high school, Emmitt ran like a pro.*

To Coach Thomas, goals like this were important.
He handed note cards to the players from time to time
and asked each one to write down his own goals.
Thomas believed that by writing one's goals on paper,
dreams became more of a reality. They became something to look at and work toward. Emmitt wrote a list of
goals and taped the list inside his locker. At the top of
the list was Emmitt's oldest and most important goal: to
one day play on the Dallas Cowboys team.

Gator Glory

Emmitt worked hard toward his goals. He ran and lifted weights every day to build his strength. When he made a mistake or had a bad game, Emmitt did not get too discouraged. Soon, he became widely known as one of Florida's top high school players. Thanks to Emmitt's winning plays, the once-pitiful Escambia Gators finished the season at seven wins and three losses. It was their first winning season in seven years.

Young All-Star

The following season, Emmitt led the Gators all the way to the state championship finals. But before the final game of the season, the star running back sprained his ankle. It ached with every step. While his coaches and doctors urged him to rest, Emmitt was determined to help the team. Hobbling on his sore ankle, Emmitt not only played but also scored a touchdown. The Escambia Gators became state champions for the very first time. They repeated this victory with a 13-0 record the next year.

In Emmitt's senior season with the Gators, Escambia was knocked out of the playoffs by rival Pensacola High School. Despite this disappointing finish, Emmitt had played well that season. He won Player of the Year honors from both *Parade* magazine and *USA Today*, and he also appeared in *Sports Illustrated*. Emmitt completed his

Emmitt runs a rope course during practice with the Arizona Cardinals in 2003. Emmitt's commitment to practice and training began in his youth.

high school career with a record of forty-five 100-yard **rushing** games, a first in Florida history.

By this time, Emmitt had become a superstar among high school players. The phone at the Smith household rang constantly with offers from college coaches. Sometimes it rang nine or ten times per night while Emmitt was doing his homework. The Smiths were concerned that all this attention would interfere with Emmitt's schoolwork. But Emmitt continued to study hard and received good grades, finishing in the top one hundred of his class.

Off to College

After visiting many colleges throughout the nation, Emmitt narrowed his choices down to two: Auburn, in Alabama, and the University of Florida, in nearby Gainesville. Emmitt ultimately chose the University of Florida, which had a stronger academic program than Auburn. Besides, Gainesville was much closer to his family in Pensacola.

Emmitt was excited to begin playing football at the University of Florida. By coincidence, the college team was called the "Gators"—the same name as Emmitt's Escambia High School team. Emmitt hoped he would be as successful in college football as he had been at Escambia High.

Emmitt spent the preseason lifting extra weights to improve his strength. He gained fifteen pounds of muscle during the summer. While Emmitt had been larger than his teammates as a child, his growth spurt had stopped at five feet nine inches. Other players now towered over

Emmitt runs during practice with the Dallas Cowboys in 1998. At five feet nine inches tall, Emmitt is shorter than most other football players.

him, and he was not as quick as he used to be. As a result, some football writers doubted Emmitt's ability. "I always heard that I was too small and too slow to be a really great football player," Emmitt later said. "But that didn't bother me, because I believed in my heart that I could be as good as anyone else. You may go through some difficult times, but things will work out for the best."[2]

Star Player

Florida coach Galen Hall had told Emmitt that he would be the starting tailback for the team. Emmitt could hardly wait. Yet when the starters were announced prior to the first game, Emmitt was not among them. In fact, he was not sent onto the field until the fourth quarter. As

Emmitt dodges two Arizona Cardinals defenders. Emmitt honed his skills while playing college football.

he watched the Gators fall behind the opposing team, Emmitt wondered why he had not been a starter. Coach Hall later explained to Emmitt that he did not want to put too much pressure on him right away. Emmitt told the coach that he was ready for the challenge. Soon he began earning more playing time.

The more Emmitt played, the better his skills became. He reached the one-thousand-yard rushing mark in just seven games, faster than any other freshman in the National Collegiate Athletic Association's (NCAA's) history. By the end of the season, Emmitt had rushed 1,341 yards. Even more impressive was the fact that, while only a freshman, he placed ninth in the voting for the Heisman Trophy. This important award is given annually to the top college football player. Many past winners, such as O.J. Simpson, Herschel Walker, and Emmitt's childhood idol, Tony Dorsett, had gone on to become pro superstars. Emmitt set his sights on winning the Heisman the following year.

Emmitt led the Gators to victories in their first five games of his sophomore season. Then, in a particularly rough game against Memphis State, Emmitt was hit from behind, tearing a ligament in his knee. It was a serious injury, and doctors were not certain how long it would take to heal. Emmitt underwent **physical therapy** with the hope of speeding up the healing process.

A Big Disappointment

Without Emmitt on the field, the Gators suddenly began losing. It was difficult for Emmitt to watch the team lose, knowing that he could not jump in and help his teammates. Finally, Emmitt convinced his doctors that he was well enough to return to play. Despite missing a few games, he had 988 rushing yards for the season. The missed games, however, were enough to put Emmitt out of contention for the Heisman Trophy. It was a big disappointment for the star running back.

Emmitt came back the following season with a strong desire to prove that he was worthy of the Heisman. He established the University of Florida's rushing record, with 1,599 yards. He was named running back on the *Sporting News* College All-America first team, and he won several other awards and honors. In the Heisman voting, however, he finished a distant seventh. Emmitt was disappointed but decided to set a new goal: to win the National Football League's (NFL's) **Rookie of the Year** honors during his first season as a pro player.

Going Pro

Around this time, several Gators players and coaches were accused of illegal acts such as gambling. Coach Hall

Emmitt gracefully breaks a tackle. In his freshman year at the University of Florida, Emmitt placed ninth in the voting for the Heisman Trophy.

Emmitt leaps over a Tampa Bay Buccaneer linebacker. While attending the University of Florida, Emmitt established a rushing record that stands today.

abruptly resigned, and four students were suspended. While Emmitt was not involved in these activities, the situation affected him as a member of the team. The Gators were placed on probation by the NCAA and were not allowed to play in **bowl games** or televised games.

That year (1990) marked the first in which NFL teams could **draft** college players other than seniors.

19

Many people asked Emmitt if he was going to declare himself eligible for the draft. Emmitt was not sure. He was anxious to begin his pro career but also knew how important it was to complete his college degree. He still had thirteen course credits left. Emmitt thought about his options, then talked it over with his parents. The Smiths supported their son's decision: He would declare himself eligible for the draft *and* he would complete his degree. To do this, he would take classes during the summer months.

Becoming a Cowboy

The 1990 NFL draft included a wealth of talented players. While Emmitt had set more than fifty-five records during his high school and college years, he was unsure about when, or whether, he would be chosen by an NFL team. Together with his family, Emmitt nervously watched the draft on television. When he was not among the first sixteen players to be chosen, Emmitt became more nervous. He could hardly bear to watch anymore. Soon, the telephone rang. When Mrs. Smith answered, Bob Ackles of the Dallas Cowboys asked to speak with Emmitt. The Cowboys, the team he had idolized since childhood, was drafting him. Emmitt's childhood dream had come true.

With that goal behind him, Emmitt began to strive for something much higher: to become the NFL's all-time leading rusher. It would not be an easy feat, but Emmitt Smith was intent on making history.

Superstar

Emmitt could hardly believe that he had been drafted by the Dallas Cowboys. The Cowboys, who had the worst rushing record in the NFL that year, were just as happy to have Emmitt on their team. With his incredible rushing skills, the Cowboys were hoping that Emmitt could help turn things around. He got his chance to play in the second game of the season, against the powerful New York Giants. Unfortunately, Emmitt was able to run the ball for only eleven yards that day, and the team lost.

Emmitt knew that he could do better for the Cowboys. He simply needed to get the ball more. Emmitt told his coaches how he felt. If the team could get the ball to him, he would take care of the rest. The coaches listened, and things began to turn around. In game four, against the Tampa Bay Buccaneers, Emmitt carried the ball twenty-three times for 123 yards. The Cowboys had their first win. From that point forward, there was a pattern. When Emmitt had the chance to carry the ball many times, the team was able to pull off a win. Otherwise, it was a losing game.

In 1990 Emmitt achieved his childhood dream of becoming a Dallas Cowboy. He was selected because of his incredible rushing skills.

The Cowboys finished that season with a record of 7-9. While it was an improvement from their previous season, it was not good enough to send the Cowboys to the playoffs. Nevertheless, Emmitt was chosen to play in his first **Pro Bowl**, and he achieved his goal of being named Rookie of the Year. "I really wanted (to be) Rookie of the Year," Emmitt later said. "I didn't win the Heisman, and I wanted to show people that questioned whether I could play at the next level, that I was for real!"[3]

Making Changes

Despite such success, Emmitt felt that some things needed to change. There was no reason why the Cowboys could not win more games. Coach Jimmy Johnson agreed. He hired a new **offensive coordinator**, Norv Turner, to help with the change. Soon, things began to come together. Emmitt carried the ball more and more, and the Cowboys began winning consistently. Emmitt rushed for 1,593 yards, winning the NFL rushing title for the 1991–1992 season. And the Cowboys made the playoffs for the first time in years.

This was an exciting time for Emmitt. While the Cowboys lost in the playoffs, the experience was a valuable one. Emmitt and his teammates became more confident with each game. The Cowboys began the 1992–1993 season with an awe-inspiring victory over the reigning **Super Bowl** champions, the Washington Redskins. They continued winning throughout the season and easily earned a berth in the 1992 playoffs. Once again, Emmitt was the NFL's leading rusher.

This time, the Cowboys were ready for their opponents. With Emmitt leading the team, they coasted over the San Francisco Forty-Niners in the National Football Conference (NFC) Championship. The team then headed to the Super Bowl, pro football's annual championship game.

Emmitt was thrilled to compete in his first Super Bowl. Fighting off his nerves, he produced 108 rushing yards and 27 yards **receiving**. The Cowboys crushed the Buffalo Bills with a final score of 52 to 17. Emmitt became the only player to win the NFL rushing title and the Super Bowl in the same season. He would repeat this accomplishment in 1993 and 1995.

Cowboys quarterback Chad Hutchinson hands off the ball to Emmitt. The Cowboys had many successful seasons as a result of Emmitt's rushing ability.

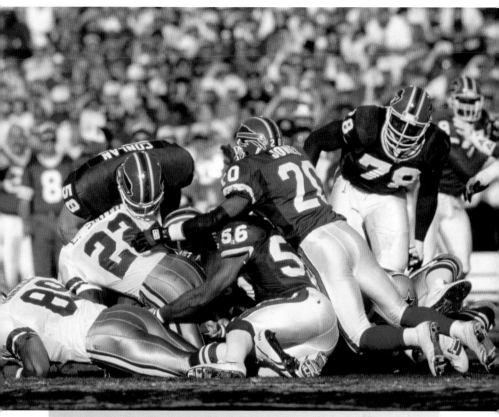

Emmitt, number twenty-two, is tackled in the 1993 Super Bowl against the Buffalo Bills. Emmitt was a key factor in the Cowboys' victory that year.

Helping Others

With all that he had achieved thus far, Emmitt remembered what his parents had taught him about helping others. He spent much of his free time working with children's charities. Emmitt donated his time to the Make-A-Wish Foundation, an organization that fulfills the wishes of children with serious illnesses, and many other charities. He often allowed kids to visit the Cowboys' practice facility during the season.

Emmitt greets children at Disneyland. Emmitt spends much of his free time working with children's charities.

Emmitt enjoyed this charity work so much that he decided to establish The Open Doors Foundation. This organization helps young people to achieve their dreams through educational and financial programs. Emmitt told *Time for Kids*, "I put a lot of my emphasis on helping kids get a better education, and we try to help open doors for children so that they can grow and learn in an environment that has nothing to do with where they live or how much money their parents have."[4]

Besides helping children in need, Emmitt continued his own college education. He did not forget the promise he had made to his parents when he first joined the

NFL. Even though Emmitt was making millions of dollars as a pro football star, he continued to take courses at the University of Florida during the summer months.

A Few Setbacks

The 1993 season began with some difficulty for Emmitt. His original three-year contract with the Cowboys had expired, and his agent was trying to work out a new deal. Emmitt thought he should receive a raise, but the Cowboys' management did not agree. It took a long time for Emmitt's agent and the team to come to terms. Emmitt missed the entire preseason and the first two regular-season games. Finally, the Cowboys agreed to the terms of the new contract.

After missing so much playing time, Emmitt could not wait to get back on the field. Well-rested and eager to win, he led the Cowboys to many victories. Then, in the final game of the regular season, Emmitt suffered a serious shoulder injury. His whole shoulder stung with pain, and his arm hung limp at his side. Nevertheless, Emmitt refused to give up. He played through the pain, leading the Cowboys to a 16-to-13 victory, in overtime, against the New York Giants. "I was an Emmitt Smith fan way before then," Giants coach Dan Reeves later said. "All that did was just solidify everything I thought about him."[5]

Emmitt followed up that stellar performance with the Cowboys' second consecutive Super Bowl victory. Emmitt was named the Super Bowl's **Most Valuable Player** (MVP) and was also voted MVP for the regular season. He also earned his third consecutive NFL rushing title.

In 1994 Emmitt experienced two major losses off the field. Coach Jimmy Johnson, who had become like a family member to Emmitt, left the Cowboys. A worse blow followed when Emmitt's beloved grandmother, Mama, died. This was an especially difficult time for Emmitt. He chose to honor his grandmother's memory by continuing to help others in need.

Dallas Cowboys coach Jimmy Johnson and Emmitt celebrate after winning a game. Emmitt and Johnson became very close friends.

New Season, New Coach

After Jimmy Johnson left the team, Barry Switzer took over as coach. After being with Coach Johnson for so many years, it took time for the Cowboys to adjust to Switzer's style. It was a good season for Emmitt, who had 1,484 rushing yards and twenty-two touchdowns. But there would be no Super Bowl for the Cowboys in 1994. They were defeated by the San Francisco Forty-Niners with a score of 38 to 28 in the NFC Championship game. Emmit worked hard to improve his skills during the off-season.

Emmitt returned in 1995 to break more records, landing twenty-five touchdowns and rushing for 1,773 yards. He led the Cowboys to their third Super Bowl win, scoring two touchdowns in the second half to defeat the Pittsburgh Steelers 27 to 17. Emmitt also continued to work toward his goal of becoming the NFL's all-time leading rusher. By 1996, he had become only the twelfth player in NFL history to top the 10,000-yard mark.

On May 1, 1996, Emmitt achieved another important goal. He graduated from the University of Florida with a bachelor of science degree. Along with his family, many of Emmitt's fans attended the ceremony to cheer for him. Accepting his degree, Emmitt proved to many people how important it is to complete one's education. "It was a promise that he made when he came out early—that he would come back and get his degree," Emmitt's mother, Mary, later said. "I'm very, very happy."[6]

Chapter Four

Making History

By 1997 Emmitt had earned four rushing titles, three Super Bowl rings, and had broken numerous football records. Many sportswriters wondered how long this success could continue. Emmitt was getting older, and his body did not seem as strong or quick as it used to be. Once again, Emmitt did not let these comments bother him. He knew that, while he was indeed getting older, he still had many great games ahead of him. Emmitt proved this on November 8, 1998, when he became the Cowboys' career rushing leader, with 12,037 yards. Each season, he gained more yards in his quest for the all-time rushing title.

The all-time rushing list read like a "who's who" of football legends. Greats such as Barry Sanders, Eric Dickerson, and Jim Brown were among the top ten. Chicago Bears superstar Walter Payton, known as

"Sweetness" for his kind personality, topped the list at 16,726 yards. Payton had retired after the 1987 season, but nobody had come close to breaking his record.

Sweetness

Emmitt had met Payton a few years back, and the two became great friends. Like Emmitt, "Sweetness" enjoyed helping children and worked with many children's

Emmitt shows off the second of his three Super Bowl rings.

charities. The Bears superstar became a mentor to Emmitt, who had looked up to him since childhood. Emmitt also became friendly with Payton's wife, Connie, and their children, Jarrett and Brittney. When Payton died of cancer in 1999, Emmitt was devastated. He remained close to the Payton family after Walter's death. In fact, he often checked in with the family to make sure

Emmitt Smith's Rushing Statistics

Year	Attempts	Yards	Touchdowns
1990	241	937	11
1991*	365	1,563	12
1992*	373	1,713	18
1993*	283	1,486	9
1994	368	1,484	21
1995*	377	1,773	25
1996	327	1,204	12
1997	261	1,074	4
1998	319	1,332	13
1999	329	1,397	11
2000	294	1,203	9
2001	261	1,021	3
2002	254	975	5
Totals	4,052	17,162	153

*NFL Rushing Champion

Source: National Football League.

they were doing well. If Connie or the children ever needed somebody to talk to, Emmitt was there.

Family had always been the most important part of Emmitt's life. By 1999, he was ready to settle down and raise a family of his own. He had been dating Patricia Lawrence, an actress and former Miss Virginia, for three years. When Pat surprised Emmitt with a party for his thirtieth birthday, Emmitt returned the surprise by asking Pat to become his wife. She accepted, and they were married the following year.

Rushing into History

On the field, Emmitt came closer to his all-time rushing goal. In a September 2001 game against San Diego, Emmitt moved past Barry Sanders, the second-leading all-time rusher. Now only Payton ranked above him. The media created a frenzy. Would Emmitt overcome his friend and mentor's all-time record and become the leading rusher in the history of the NFL?

Many people seemed to think so. The media, fans, and the Cowboys franchise encouraged Emmitt in his quest. The team purchased billboards that read, "Run, Emmitt, Run." Emmitt's photo was printed on Cowboys' game tickets. Emmitt himself decided to take the opportunity to continue with his charity work. He created a campaign called "Helping Emmitt Help Kids." The goal of this effort was to raise 22 million dollars for America's schools while Emmitt attempted to capture the rushing title.

On October 27, 2002, a crowd of 63,854 gathered in Texas Stadium to watch the Cowboys take on the Seattle

Emmitt and his wife Pat pose at the 2003 ESPY Awards.
Emmitt and Pat dated for four years before marrying in 2000.

Seahawks. Included in this crowd were Eddie Payton, Walter's brother, and several members of the Smith family. This was not just an ordinary game. It was history in the making. "[Walter] once said that if anybody breaks his record, he hopes it is Emmitt because he would do it with the class and the dignity that the record represents,"[7] Eddie Payton told ESPN.

Top Ten Lifetime Rushers*

Player	Years of Career	Yards	Touchdowns
Emmitt Smith	13	17,162	153
Walter Payton	13	16,726	110
Barry Sanders	10	15,269	99
Eric Dickerson	11	13,259	90
Tony Dorsett	12	12,739	77
Jim Brown	9	12,312	106
Marcus Allen	16	12,243	123
Franco Harris	13	12,120	91
Thurman Thomas	13	12,074	65
Jerome Bettis	10	11,542	62

*as of the start of the 2003 season

Source: Pro Football Hall of Fame.

Emmitt began the game by running for 62 yards on his first eleven carries. Then, in the fourth quarter, he ran for the eleven yards that brought his career-rushing total to 16,743—17 yards more than Walter Payton's all-time record. Emmitt Smith was now the all-time leading rusher. A colorful banner celebrating Emmitt's accomplishment was unfurled from the roof of the stadium. A televised message from Connie Payton to Emmitt lit up on the overhead screen. The crowd went wild.

"Then they stopped the game, and I went over and hugged my mom," Emmitt later said. "And that made me cry. Moms make you feel that way at special times in your life. Then I saw my wife and my kids, and I hugged them. I thought about Walter Payton before the next play, and I said a little prayer for him. I felt like he was watching. I know he was watching."[8]

Leaving the Cowboys

With the rushing title came many other awards and honors for Emmitt. He received the Walter Payton Spirit of Sweetness award, which is given to a person who sets an example by giving to others. Emmitt also received a congratulatory phone call from President George W. Bush. In October 2002 Emmitt's picture was featured on the Wheaties cereal box.

As the all-time rushing leader, many wondered if Emmitt would retire from football. The Cowboys had a new coach, Bill Parcells, who was focused on bringing in some new, young players. Emmitt's contract was due to expire, and his future with the Cowboys was uncertain.

Emmitt accepts an award at the 2003 ESPY Awards. Emmitt made football history when he broke the NFL rushing record in 2002.

Now approaching thirty-four years of age, Emmitt was no longer as fast or strong as he used to be.

On February 27, 2003, Emmitt volunteered to be released from the Cowboys. It was a sad moment for the star, who had worn a Cowboys uniform for thirteen years. But Emmitt knew that it was time for him to move on. He wanted to leave the team just as he had played, with class and dignity. The following month, Emmitt signed a two-year contract with the Arizona Cardinals.

"I still love the game, and I still know that I can play," Emmitt said. "I am thankful that this organization saw some of the things I was able to do and believed in me, giving me the opportunity to show that to the world."[9]

As he settles into his new career in Arizona, Emmitt continues to enjoy the most important things in his life: his wife and children. Emmitt's favorite role is playing dad to his two young daughters, Rheagen and Jasmin, and his baby son, Emmitt IV, known as E.J. In his free time, Emmitt enjoys playing golf, and often challenges his teammates to another of his favorite games: dominoes.

Emmitt Smith has earned a place as one of the greatest players in football history. Even more important, he has touched the world with his kindness and great respect for others. Of course, Emmitt would not have achieved so much if he had not dared to follow his dreams. "I told my dad I was going to be a running back for the Dallas Cowboys when I was six years old," Emmitt says. "I am living proof that dreams do come true."[10]

Notes

Chapter One: A Star Is Born
1. Quoted in Jim Reeves, "For Love or Glory," *Ft. Worth Star-Telegram*, February 23, 1994, p. 1.

Chapter Two: Gator Glory
2. Quoted in Angelique Ledoux, "Emmitt Smith: All-Time Career Rusher," *Time for Kids* online, "SPORTS NEWS," October 30, 2002. www.timeforkids.com.

Chapter Three: Superstar
3. Quoted in Rudy Klancnik, *Emmitt: Run with History.* Dallas, TX: The Calvert Group, 2002, p. 70.
4. Quoted in Angelique Ledoux, "Emmitt Smith: All-Time Career Rusher."
5. Quoted in Jaime Aron, "Smith Proved Mettle in 1993 Finale," *Holland Online Sentinel*, October 23, 2002. www.hollandsentinel.com.
6. Quoted in John Lester, "More than Thirty-Two Hundred Expected to Participate in UF's Spring Graduation," *Florida University News*, May 1, 1996, p. 30.

Chapter Four: Making History

7. Quoted in Kris Schwartz, "Emmitt Gives New Meaning to Sweetness," ESPN.com, March 2003. www.espn.com.

8. Quoted in Angelique Ledoux, "Emmitt Smith: All-Time Career Rusher."

9. Quoted in Mike Rabun, "New Start for Emmitt in Arizona," Dallas Cowboys Official Weekly Website, March 2003. www.dallascowboysweekly.com

10. Quoted in Klancnik, *Emmitt: Run with History*, p. 55.

Glossary

bowl games: Postseason games for college teams.

draft: The annual process in which college players are chosen for professional teams.

housing project: A publicly built and operated housing development, usually intended for low- or moderate-income tenants.

Most Valuable Player: The player judged to be the most important in a game, or in a season.

offensive coordinator: A member of the coaching staff who is in charge of the offense.

physical therapy: Treatment for an injury by massage, exercise, or other methods without surgery or medicine.

Pro Bowl: The annual all-star game of the NFL, played each year in Hawaii.

receiving: The act of catching, or trying to catch, a forward pass.

Rookie of the Year: The player judged to be the most successful in his first year of professional play.

running back: A football player who has the responsibility of moving the ball by running with it. A running back is primarily a ball carrier.

rushing: In football, to move the ball by running.

Super Bowl: The annual championship football game between the best team of the National Football Conference and that of the American Football Conference.

touchdown: Worth six points, this is when a player has the ball in the opponent's end zone.

For Further Exploration

Books

Matt Christopher, *On the Field with Emmitt Smith*. Boston, MA: Little, Brown, 1997. Includes information on Emmitt's childhood and career through 1997.

John Grabowski, *Emmitt Smith: Sports Great*. Springfield, NJ: Enslow, 1998. Includes biography and Emmitt's career statistics through 1998.

Rudy Klancnik, *Emmitt: Run with History*. Dallas, TX: The Calvert Group, 2002. Photos, quotations, and detailed information following Emmitt's all-time rushing record.

Roland Lazenby, *Emmitt Smith: Record Breaking Rush to Glory*. Chicago, IL: Triumph Books, 2002. Includes recent information on Emmitt's career, including his breaking the all-time rushing record.

Internet Sources

ESPN.com, "Emmitt Smith." http://sports.espn.go.com. An excellent resource for Emmitt's current statistics.

NFL.com, "Emmitt Smith." www.nfl.com. Includes Emmitt's career highlights, statistics, and biographical information.

Websites

Arizona Cardinals Official Website (www.arizonacardinals.com). Offers up-to-date information on Emmitt's career with the Arizona Cardinals.

Dallas Cowboys Tribute to Emmitt Smith (www.totalcowboys.com). Includes high school, college, and Cowboys statistics and links to other Emmitt sites.

Emmitt Zone: Emmitt Smith's Official Website (www.emmittzone.com). Includes statistics, biography, photos, fun facts, news, and licensed merchandise.

Index

Picture Credits

Cover image: © Getty Images

© AFP/CORBIS, 8, 10, 11

AP/Wide World Photos, 13, 19, 22, 24, 26, 28, 31

Mike Blake/Reuters/Landov, 37

© S. Carmona/CORBIS, 25

Getty Images, 15, 16, 34

Chris Jouan, 7, 32, 35

Jeff Mitchell/Reuters/Landov, 5, 18

About the Author

Kimberly A. Gatto is the author of *Michelle Kwan: Champion on Ice* (Lerner, 1998) and *An Apple a Day: A Heartwarming Collection of True Horse Stories* (Half Halt Press, 2000). She is currently at work on a children's biography of football star Tom Brady. A lifelong equestrian, Gatto is the proud owner of two horses.